WALK
MORETO

by
John Abbott

The Duck Pond, Moreton in Marsh

CONTENTS

		Page
1.	Introduction.	3
2.	Town Map	5
3.	Walk 1 Moreton-in-Marsh walk plus town guide	6
4	Walk 2 Batsford, Bourton-on-the-Hill and Sezincote	13
5.	Walk 3 Dorn and Lower Lemington.	18
6.	Walk 4 Evenlode and the Four Shires Stone.	21

Published by
REARDON PUBLISHING
56, Upper Norwood Street, Leckhampton
CHELTENHAM, GL53 0DU
Website: www.reardon.co.uk
Email: reardon@bigfoot.com

"I would like to thank the Stewarts for their support."
ISBN 1 873877 63 3

Test Walked and updated by Bob Cox

Cover Photos: Redesdale Hall and Town Stocks

Cover Design and Cover Photos by Nicholas Reardon

Photography by Nicholas Reardon and David Medcroft

Drawings and Illustrations by Peter T. Reardon

Book Layout and Design by Nicholas Reardon

Printed by
STOATE & BISHOP (PRINTERS) LTD,
Cheltenham, Gloucestershire.

INTRODUCTION

Situated on the edge of the Cotswold Hills, Moreton-in-Marsh has much to offer the discerning visitor: assuredly, a sense of history and the opportunity for healthy exercise amid superb scenery.

Today, one may see traces of a Roman military camp just north of the road to Batsford. Moreover, the remains of a Roman settlement endures near Dorn; but underground this time. They were constructed soon after A.D. 43, as the Roman army took control of what is today Gloucestershire, building their forts and roads. The Fosse Way, one such road, here the A429, passes along High Street, bisecting the town.

Moreton-in-Marsh is a remarkable name, and one to remember. The 'ton' comes from the Saxon, broadly meaning a town or village - an enclosed place, a moor town, originally located in marshy ground. Several names are recorded, for example: eleventh century 'Mortune' and fifteenth century 'Moreton Henmarsh', changing with time.

Domesday Book records Moreton-in-Marsh as being in the Gloucestershire Hundred of Deerhurst when, as 'Moretune', it came under the domain of the Abbey of St Peter of Westminster. A charter for a market and then a fair was granted in the thirteenth century. The market is still held every Tuesday, when High Street overflows with stalls and people.

Four walks are described: the first is a relaxed wander around the town, an opportunity to admire the rich fabric, the weathered Cotswold stone of the buildings that line the streets. Please give a thought to traffic, particularly at the two roundabouts. The second walk perambulates to the west to look at Batsford's village church and the nearby Arboretum and Falconry Center. The falconry displays are very popular and the Center is well worth a visit. Next, it ranges south to Bourton-on-the-Hill, where stands another church (complete with Winchester Bushel and Peck) and much eye-catching housing. Later, domed Sezincote is noted in passing, though one may visit at certain times of the year. Walk 3 consists of two short and easy linear sections: first advancing to Dorn, and then (if you wish) crossing the former Stratford and Moreton Tramway to Lower Lemington for a look at a small Norman church that runs on candlepower. The fourth walk, which includes a linear option to the Four Shires Stone, saunters south to browse fourteenth century St Edward's at Evenlode.

Dress appropriately before embarking on Walks 2 - 4. Pack a waterproof - select boots that have been worn a few times, proven 'blister free'. There are hardly any gradients, but a generous helping of mud in the wetter months, and a stile or two.

Respect the countryside: guard against risk of fire; stay on the paths; keep dogs under control; do not disturb livestock; close gates (unless obviously meant to be open); avoid damage to crops, fences, hedges, trees; leave no litter; and take care of yourself, especially along roads, using the pavement or grass verge.

Maps: O.S. Landranger 151. O.S. Explorer 45.

Access: Moreton-in-Marsh lies where the A429 meets the A44 - at approximate Landranger ref: 205325. The nearest motorway point would be junction 9 of the M5. See Public Transport for the more convenient rail option.

Parking: Alongside High Street, except on a Tuesday - Market Day - when you will have to improvise. Alternatively, at quieter times, go north along High Street, moving ahead at the first roundabout, to the second roundabout, where you should see a Parking sign that directs right, along the A44, signed Oxford. Further, another 'P' points left along Station Road. The small (shoppers) car park, is on the left.

Public Transport: Bus stops are beside the Redesdale Hall. There is a railway station situated to the east of the north end of High Street, off Station Road, saving the 'wear and tear' of a drive.

Start: The walks start at the Redesdale Hall (see Cover Picture) on the west side of High Street.

Refreshments: There are so many inns, tea rooms and restaurants that one is spoilt for choice.

Public Toilets: Gents by the Redesdale Hall. Ladies a few yards away along Corders Lane.

TIC: Tourist Information Centre is on the east side of High Street (the oppersite side of the road to Redesdate Hall) in the Council Offices.

Moreton in Marsh
Town Map

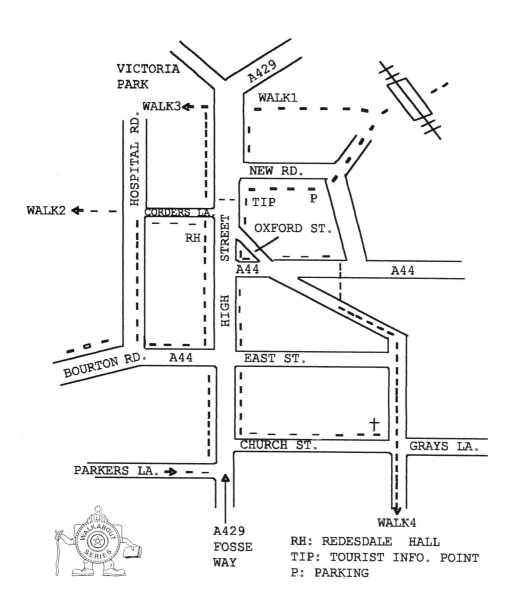

VICTORIA PARK

A429

WALK3

WALK1

HOSPITAL RD.

NEW RD.

WALK2

CORDERS LA.

TIP

P

OXFORD ST.

STREET

RH

HIGH

A44

A44

BOURTON RD.

A44

EAST ST.

CHURCH ST.

GRAYS LA.

PARKERS LA.

WALK4

A429
FOSSE
WAY

RH: REDESDALE HALL
TIP: TOURIST INFO. POINT
P: PARKING

WALK 1

Moreton in Marsh (Town Guide Walk)

Route: Redesdale Hall - Bourton Road - Hospital Road - Corders Lane - High Street - Railway Station - New Road - High Street - Curfew Tower - Oxford Street - Church Street - High Street - Redesdale Hall.

Distance / time: Variable - a wander within the town.

Standing beside: The Redesdale Hall

The focal point of the town and built in 1887, the year of the Golden Jubilee of Queen Victoria, by Mr AB Freeman Mitford. In 1905, he was made First Baron Redesdale, the same year in which he entertained his friend, King Edward VII, at Batsford. Memorials to the Freeman and Mitford families may be seen in Batsford's Church of St Mary during Walk 2. Looking up at first floor level, one can see the Mitford coat of arms in the windows; also in stone on the south side. The roofing slates of Cotswold stone lead the eye to a fine clock tower. Antique Fairs are often held inside the hall.

THE WALK

Now go south, along the west side of High Street, only a few yards to:

The Redesdale Arms

One of the former coach inns of the town that dates from the end of the eighteenth century. The entrance to the Archway Bar leads to where a pig market was held.

Onward, soon turning right into Bourton Road to the start of Hospital Road which is on the right-hand side. Here, one may continue along Bourton Road for a couple of minutes, crossing with care to:

The Wellington Aviation Museum

The museum was established by Gerry Tyack, a former Engine Fitter with the RAF. He has raised thousands of pounds for RAF funds. There used to be a World War Two airfield (to the east of the town) which trained

Wellington crews. Gerry, calling upon his service with the RAF, has built up an interesting collection of aviation art and miscellanea that focuses on the Vickers Armstrong Wellington bomber. The museum is open daily except Mondays.

Return to the start of Hospital Road; the house, Three Ways, stands at the corner. Take this road as far as Corders Lane. Opposite, a posted metal walker points west, the route adopted by the Batsford Walk. But you go right - Corders Lane to High Street - next, moving by way of the Pedestrian Crossing to the other side. The Council Offices and Tourist Information are nearby. Now bear left along High Street, taking pleasure in the housing, and having no problem with the date cut in the stone of diminutive White Lion Cottage which at one time was a public house. Adjacent Lloyds Bank is also eighteenth century. It has an imposing, pedimental doorway, a column on either side and, with walkers in mind, scrapers for the boots.

Advance to just before the Supermarket. Follow the sign that points to a public footpath on the right, curving east to south, and where the path continues via a footbridge over the railway line, go straight ahead, passing to the right of:

The Railway Station

The Railway Station

Lucky Moreton: one of the few Cotswold towns to have an open railway station - part of the Cotswold Line between Oxford, Worcester. The railway arrived in the 1850s. Prior to this date, there existed a tramway between Stratford-upon-Avon and Moreton-in-Marsh (opened 1826); subsequently, horse-drawn wagons carried goods to and fro, soon to be replaced by steam power.

At the corner - a car park is opposite - bear right passing Royal British Legion building along New Road, past the substantial Post Office (opened 1933), to High Street, again.

Turn left, retracing part of your earlier route, eventually passing narrow Oxford Street to the corner and the busy A44. Here stands:

The Curfew Tower

Quite possibly dating from the sixteenth century and still with a bell that was rung, every morning and evening, until 1860. There used to be a lock-up in the bell tower. On this west side, close to an old studded door, a notice dated August 5th, 1905, defines 'The Undermentioned Tolls' for markets and fairs. Additionally, there is a clock on the south side.

The Curfew Tower

Go left, here, walking in an easterly direction along the left-hand pavement of the A44, coming to:

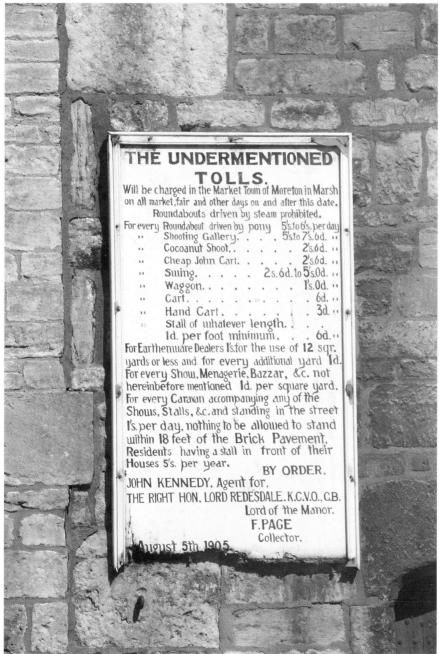

THE UNDERMENTIONED TOLLS.

Will be charged in the Market Town of Moreton in Marsh on all market, fair and other days on and after this date.

Roundabouts driven by steam prohibited.

For every Roundabout driven by pony   5's.to 6's. per day
        Shooting Gallery. . . .   5's.to 7's.6d. ''
        Cocoanut Shoot. . . . .   2's.6d. ''
        Cheap John Cart. . . . .   2's.6d. ''
        Swing. . . . .   2s.6d. to 5's.0d. ''
        Waggon. . . . .   1's.0d. ''
        Cart. . . . .   6d. ''
        Hand Cart. . . . .   3d. ''
        Stall of whatever length. . .
        1d. per foot minimum, . . 6d. ''

For Earthenware Dealers 1's.for the use of 12 sqr. yards or less and for every additional yard 1d. For every Show, Menagerie, Bazzar, &c. not hereinbefore mentioned 1d. per square yard. For every Caravan accompanying any of the Shows, Stalls, &c. and standing in the street 1's. per day, nothing to be allowed to stand within 18 feet of the Brick Pavement. Residents having a stall in front of their Houses 5's. per year.

BY ORDER.

JOHN KENNEDY. Agent for,

THE RIGHT HON. LORD REDESDALE. K.C.V.O., C.B.

Lord of the Manor.

F.PAGE
Collector.

August 5th 1905.

Old Sign on the Curfew Tower

The Mann Institute

Erected in 1891 by Miss Edith Mann in memory of her father, Dr John Mann. See the quote by John Ruskin, the art and social critic, above the door, and further, beneath the window, an inscribed tablet telling you that this was: 'The birthplace of John Mann 1802-1885 ...' At this point stop awhile to admire the tower and the fine gable end which draws the eye.

The Mann Institute

On the other side of the road is Lemington House, which has sixteenth and eighteenth century features. Bear left beyond the Institute.

Continue down Oxford Street to view more attractive housing, for example: Greystones, Town House, and The Cottage. Further, is The Old School House, with large lettering in stone: 'Infant School established 1851'.

At Roseville, by the start of Station Road, cross street with considerable care, going left a few yards and down the brick steps to the end of Oxford Street. Follow the road as it curves south - St David's School playing fields are to the left - threading between railings and forging ahead. Pausing here, in Old Town, seventeenth century Lilac Cottage is one of several houses deserving of attention.

Proceed to the crossroads (Gray's Lane is on the left), turning right into Church Street and:

The Church of St David:

While walking along the churchyard path, look up at the battlemented tower exhibiting four huge pinnacles topped by an octagonal spire that reaches to 116 feet overall. With likely origins in Saxon times, the church has undergone many refurbishments and additions in later centuries. Until the 1880s, it was a chapel-of-ease to Bourton-on-the-Hill. Enter via the door in the west tower. Here, to the background 'tick-tock' of the clock, one may read the lettering on the north side telling you that St David's was restored in 1858 and the tower rebuilt in 1861.

Information bats and a booklet: 'The Vale of Moreton Churches', by Guy Stapleton, are available; both describe the church much better than yours truly. The latter can be used when visiting other churches in the area. Lofty-arched arcades run either side of the nave. The pulpit is to the left, at the eastern end. Move to the south side, where stands the font, to return west along the south aisle. On the wall you will see several photographs and plans of the church.

Leaving, bear right, to High Street. The seventeenth century Manor House Hotel is on the corner. At this point, if you wish, brave the traffic for a look at what is known as University Farm. The moulding above the door, with 16 and 78 on either side, is strong on eye-appeal. It is called Campion House, now. Recalling the Mann Institute quote - Ruskin House is on one side.

Back by the Manor House Hotel, go north along the right-hand side of High Street, coming to:

The White Hart Royal Hotel:

The building once served as a coach inn and is believed to date from the seventeenth century. By all accounts, King Charles I stopped here in 1644. Looking through the entrance, one can still see a cobbled strip running from door to door.

Finally, cross the A44 with care, making use of the traffic island, returning via the Pedestrian Crossing to the Redesdale Hall.

The Church of St David, Moreton in Marsh

WALK 2

Batsford, Bourton on the Hill & Sezincote

Route: Redesdale Hall - Corders Lane - path west to 'walk crossroads' - linear option to Batsford village - Batsford Arboretum - Bourton-on-the-Hill - Sezincote - Redesdale Hall.

Distance / time: Up to 8 miles and 4 hours plus browsing time.

THE WALK

At the Redesdale Hall, go a few yards north, then left along Corders Lane to the T-junction and Hospital Road, taking the signed footpath opposite, direction west.

The Redesdale Hall Clock Tower

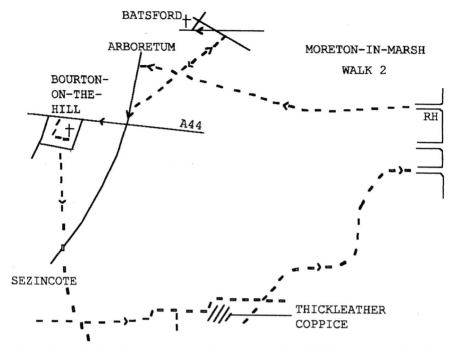

BATSFORD

ARBORETUM

MORETON-IN-MARSH

WALK 2

BOURTON-
ON-THE-
HILL

A44

RH

SEZINCOTE

THICKLEATHER
COPPICE

Pass through the kissing-gate and across the first field. Approaching the hedge, veer to the right, slightly, approximately north-west. Later, an arrow-head on a post directs left to a gate, where you next bear right along a strip of grass. A succession of arrow-heads and gates across fields two to five follow, heading a point north of west. The opposing hedge of the fifth field has mostly gone, as you move into the sixth field and on beyond its far right-hand corner, keeping the wire fencing to your right, soon crossing a small stone footbridge. Walk north-west, eventually reaching a chained gate and advancing to another kissing-gate. One of the discs defines the 'Heart of England Way'.

Continue to a walkers' signpost - the 'walk crossroads' - with options of: bearing right, to Batsford village and church; going ahead to look at the Batsford Arboretum and Falconry Centre; or bearing left, south-west, across the field to a stile and Bourton-on-the-Hill.

Selecting the first option: go right, north-east. Making progress and nearing the end of the third field, on the left, in the distance, you can see nineteenth century Batsford House. Onward, enjoying grassy walking and fine views, negotiating several stiles, to the road.

Turn left, and left again at the crossroads, signed: 'Batsford Village'. Further, if you wish, take the right-hand road to Batsford Stud. The nineteenth century building is worth the extra walk, particularly to view (from the road) the oriel window above the entrance, crowned by a gable. Retracing, go right, on to:

The Church of St Mary

St Mary's is generally closed in the winter months when prior notice of a visit is appreciated. Keys may be obtained nearby.

Mount these steps into the churchyard to acknowledge the apsidal feature of the chancel. Move around to the west side, noting the tower and spire, with an octagonal drum and four sizable pinnacles.

Enter via the door in the tower and then the left-hand door. At this west end is a wooden screen and the Batsford Park pew. Immediately to the right, on a shelf, are information bats and Guy Stapleton's booklet. Both describe the church much better than this brief summary. Ahead is the font, and beyond, on the north side, a richly decorated marble coffin lid with lettering: 'Honourable Frances Elizabeth Mitford' on the side. The booklet tells you about her generosity concerning the rebuilding of the church in the 1860s.

Walk east along the nave. Memorials to the Freeman and Mitford families are everywhere. For example, on the north wall, one with columns and a pediment, to the first Lord Redesdale: 'In memory of John Lord Redesdale born August 18th 1748, died January 16th 1830 ... also in memory of Frances Lady Redesdale born December 4th 1767, died August 22nd 1817 ...' Further, is an angel in white marble, in memory of the first Lord's son: 'In this church lies buried John Thomas Freeman-Mitford Earl of Redesdale ... born Sept.9 1805 died May 2 1886.'

Internally, the chancel is most attractive: the aforementioned apsidal feature, vaulting above, and four nineteenth century stained glass windows.

Leaving, retrace to the 'walk crossroads'. From here, the route to the arboretum is simply described: facing the signpost, proceed left, north-west, to the road. The Heart of England Way continues ahead, but you go right, to:

Batsford Arboretum and Falconry Centre

A descriptive leaflet may be obtained from the centre or from the towns tourist centre:

The Arboretum reveals a strong Japanese influence and is particularly eye-catching in spring and autumn.

The Falconry Centre fascinates young and old alike, but especially children, even keeping them quiet for a while.

Continue south along the road's grass verge, making for Bourton-on-the-Hill and Sezincote. The south-west route joins on the left.

At the A44, the entrance to Sezincote is opposite. A notice advises when the Gardens and House are open.

Bear right, progressing the tarmac path to Bourton-on-the-Hill. Further, on the left, stands an old barn. There is a stone with 1570 cut into it above the massive door. Next comes a roadside view of Bourton House, which has origins in the sixteenth century.

Later, on the left, is a building displaying lettering: 'The Retreat for the Aged erected 1831'. If you have already crossed, be wary of a few yards of non-pavement while finding time for the charming cottages on either side: appropriately, Rambler Cottage and lucky Horseshoe Cottage, for example. Now take the road on the left, and opposite Tawnies, climb the steps, strolling through the churchyard, around to the north porch of:

The Church of St Laurence

According to a keyholder, the church is 'generally open'. Beyond and above the porch, a line of gargoyles stare down.

Inside, on a nearby shelf, Parish Notes may be purchased for a few pence. There is also an information bat; as ever, describing the church much better than yours truly. The bat will tell you that the church dates from Norman times when it was dedicated to St Mary the Virgin. Steps on the right lead up to what's left of a gallery. The fifteenth century octagonal font is nearby.

Walk along the north aisle. Part of the stained glass of the east window is also fifteenth century. The bat gives the detail. Move to the end of the nave and look west to see: on one side, the round Norman piers of the older south arcade; on the other, the hexagonal piers of the fourteenth century north arcade, clerestory above.

Within the chancel are riddel posts around the altar and a piscina in the south window. The Winchester Bushel and Peck are by the entrance. At the east end of the south aisle is a fourteenth century stone screen.

Emerging via the north porch, first go to the A44 to see seventeenth century Sundial Cottage, opposite. The Horse and Groom is further up the road. This eighteenth century public house, offers a respectable pint of draught Bass (wet and hoppy), nourishment and a log fire in the winter.

Now retrace back through the churchyard, down the steps to the road off the A44, this time bearing right, following the road as it curves right by the telephone box, to a path on the left, signed Sezincote and Longborough. Take this path, direction roughly south. The unsurfaced lane soon gives way to three fields and gates (to be closed), a stile, fourth field and two kissing-gates. A fifth field is crossed by the lane that leads to Sezincote. However, you go ahead, fencing funnelling through a gap between trees, to a sixth field. Here, on the right, you can see early nineteenth century Sezincote, at least in part. The green, copper dome attracts the eye.

Advance to field 7 and then to a narrow metalled lane. There is a cattle-grid on right. Bear left, east: the start of a long stretch, with a bend or two, passing Upper Rye Farm, and ahead, as directed by the arrow-head (another points right, but ignore). The tarmac disappears as you proceed east into the field, following the tyre tracks. Rounding Thickleather Coppice, strike east, again, to where you should come to a short post with an arrow-head and bear left, slightly, making for a gate in the far hedge (not staying east towards a stile).

Beyond, move into the left-hand field, walking a point east of north, keeping the hedge to your right, attaining the corner and stepping into the next field. Upper Fields Farm lies further to the left. A series of fields have yet to be traversed, to a spot where you heed the yellow public footpath sign that points left. Onward, eventually reaching a gate that currently must be climbed. Approaching housing, the tarmac of Parkers Lane is joined, shortly passing the ambulance and fire stations, to High Street. The duck pond is at the corner, a watering-hole for horses not too long ago. Now turn left, traffic wary, back to the Redesdale Hall.

WALK 3

Dorn and Lower Lemington

Route: Redesdale Hall - Victoria Park - Dorn - Lower Lemington - optional circular route passing close to Aston Magna - Dorn - Redesdale Hall.

Distance/time: Moreton to Lower Lemington extends to around 2 miles and an easy hour, one-way; plus church browsing.

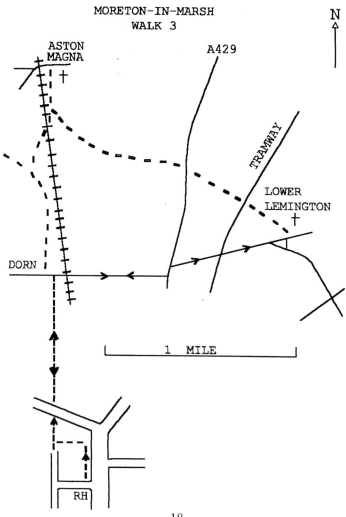

THE WALK

From the Redesdale Hall, walk north along High Street, continuing past the War Memorial, that remembers those who gave their lives in the two World Wars. Further, at a point roughly opposite the store, (Supermarket), take the signed public footpath on the left, direction west, descending steps and cutting across Victoria Park, which commemorates Queen Victoria's Diamond Jubilee of 1897. At the crossing path, go right, to the gate and Batsford road.

The War Memorial

Cross with care to the signed path, opposite. At the start of this field, and to the left, are the remains of a Roman military camp; a low bank, only. Strike north, moving into a second field near the far left-hand corner, at the end of which you pass through the metal gate (please close) and into a third field, soon emerging onto a lane to a T-junction and Dorn.

Here, one may simply retrace to Moreton, or turn right, east, passing Old Farm and New Farm (B & B). A field to the east of Old Farm contains, underground, the remains of a Roman settlement. Nothing is visible, but the farmer is not allowed to plough too deeply.

Proceed along this mostly quiet and narrow road (with grass verge) to the A429 and then go left for about 80 yards, crossing carefully, taking the road signed: 'Lower Lemington'. After a couple of minutes, you cross the former Stratford and Moreton Tramway. A line of trees marks the route. You should also see the sign: 'Crossing Cottage' on one side.

Later, leave the road where it curves right, going ahead along a lane, passing to the right of thatched Michaelmas House to:

The Church of St Leonard

St Leonard's has origins in Norman times and was extensively restored in the nineteenth century, especially internally, as you will see; though not too clearly, for it runs on candlepower.

Inside and immediately on the right, are a stoup and box inviting donations to the church restoration fund. Walk east along the nave - roofing timbers above. The wording of the stained glass in the north wall: '... take up thy bed and walk,' seems apposite.

Stand at the chancel entrance and observe the Royal Arms of George III (1815) above the arch; also the eighteenth century wooden pulpit and two squints. One has a pot of yellow primroses in it; in March, anyway.

Enter the chancel: on the right is a Norman tub-shaped font, and close to it a wooden chest on top of which should be the Church Guide and Greetings Cards; astute purchases. The guide is an interesting read; it has a sketch by Anne Clarke and poem by Catherine Meadows. Between the two lancets on the north side is an inscribed brass to: '... Charles Grevill and Peter Grevill ... ANNO DNI 1636'. The guide gives more detail.

Emerge, once more, to the bright light of day. To the south-east is the site of the medieval village of Upper Lemington. Read all about it on page 2 of the church guide.

Now, one may simply retrace to Moreton, or try the circular route that passes close to Aston Magna and rejoins this walk at Dorn. Regarding the latter: two tracks pass to the left of (facing) Michaelmas House; take the 'leftmost' that goes north-west across the field; mentioned only, not described.

WALK 4

Evenlode and The Four Shires Stone

Route: Redesdale Hall - Church Street - linear option to the Four Shires Stone - mainly southerly route to Evenlode - partial retrace - Redesdale Hall.

Distance / time: About 6 miles and 3 hours, plus church browsing.

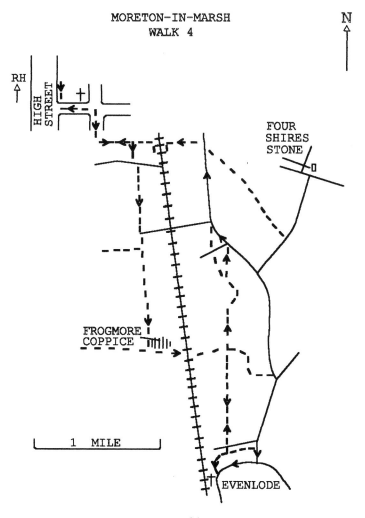

THE WALK

Leaving the Redesdale Hall, proceed via the nearby Pedestrian Crossing to the far side of High Street, next, bearing right, eventually turning left into Church Street.

Further, select the road (Old Town) on the right, opposite St David's, direction south, curving east, soon narrowing to a tarmac path. At the corner by the allotments, at Lampost with number 3 on it take the right-hand path. But first, consider: going ahead at this point would be the start of a linear option to:

The Four Shires Stone

Originally the location of four bordering counties: Oxfordshire, Warwickshire, Gloucestershire and Worcestershire, and with their names inscribed, one on each side. Worcestershire 'slipped away' in the 1930s. According to the information bat in Evenlode's church, the Stone: '... marks the place where a battle was fought about 1016 between the English and the Danes ...'

The route is a mix of fields and roads (some grass verge, some traffic - take care); mentioned and noted on the map, but not described.

Onward to Evenlode by way of the tarmac path, direction south. At the road, cross to the path opposite, shortly curving left, around the back of housing, over the footbridge and across the field.

Traverse several fields, maintaining a general southerly direction, passing to the left of Frogmore Farm and to the right of Frogmore Coppice, coming finally to a path/bridleway T-junction. You should see a railway sleeper bristling with blue and yellow arrow-heads and turn left, east, on over the railway line, reaching a post and more arrow-heads. This is the 'walk crossroads'; remember for later.

For now, bear right, 'fielding' south, ultimately to where a pair of stiles in the right-hand hedge lead you to a last stile and lane. Go left, east, to the road, then right - a short stretch to be negotiated with care. Follow the road around to the right, signed Broadwell and Adlestrop, entering Evenlode. Where the bridleway emerges stands:

The Church of St Edward

Walk along the churchyard, observing the battlemented tower, making for the south porch of this essentially fourteenth century church. Inside, on a nearby table, is a notice that welcomes you: '... we are grateful for the help and generosity of visitors ...' Currently, there is an information bat on the sill of a south window.

Move under an arch of the arcade to the nave. On the left, in the south wall, is an aumbry. Further west, stands the sculpted, octagonal font. Approaching the chancel - see the tiny wooden heads of the oak pulpit. A second aumbry is set in a west wall of the chancel.

Return to the nave and go south: part of the rood stairs remain. On the south side, are an old millstone, a piscina in the sill of one of the windows and a notice describing Nine Men's Morris. Against the wall is a stone sedile. The notes describe the adjacent window with medieval stained glass at its top; the head of Edward the Confessor. The son of Ethelred II, he was King of England from 1042, died in 1066 and was canonised in 1161.

Now retrace to the 'walk crossroads', through gate and going ahead, north, across field 1. Summarising: aim to pass through 2 trees, negotiate a stile and footbridge into field 2; cross the ditch into field 3; through a small wooden gate to field 4; climb the stile in the left-hand hedge to field 5. Two gates and a bridge of railway sleepers lead to field 6, a post and two arrow-heads. This is where the path splits in two: Chose right hand path continue right ahead, progressing by means of a metal gate in wooden fencing, seeking the diagonally opposite corner of field 7, to the road, again.

Turn left: the start of ten minutes' easy walking with plenty of grass verge. Eventually, housing begins and a signed path crosses (part of the Four Shires Stone route). Bear left along this path, between the allotments, (Very BOGGY in wet weather) across grass and a footbridge. Tracking deviously over the railway line, the path, tarmac now, soon brings you to the point where you previously turned right towards Evenlode. Go ahead, retracing to the Redesdale Hall.

The Town Stocks near to Redesdale Hall.